THE EDWARDIANS IN PHOTOGRAPHS

FRONTISPIECE   Old-style outdoor photography at the seaside, c. 1900.

THE
EDWARDIANS
in photographs

Paul Thompson & Gina Harkell

HM

HOLMES & MEIER PUBLISHERS, INC.
New York

To Charlie and To Hannah

First published in the United States of America 1979 by
HOLMES & MEIER PUBLISHERS, INC.
30 Irving Place, New York, N.Y. 10003

Copyright © 1979 Paul Thompson and Gina Harkell

Library of Congress Cataloging in Publication Data
Main entry under title:

The Edwardians in photographs.

  1. Great Britain—Social life and customs—20th
century—Pictorial works. 2. Great Britain—Social
life and customs—19th century—Pictorial works.
3. Great Britain—Social conditions—20th century—
Pictorial works. 4. Great Britain—Social conditions—
19th century—Pictorial works. I. Thompson, Paul
Richard, 1935–   II. Harkell, Gina.
DA566.4.E35 1979   779′.9′94108   79-9268
ISBN 0-8419-0529-0

ISBN 0-8419-0529-0

PRINTED IN GREAT BRITAIN

CONTENTS

Acknowledgements

Note The quotations in the text are principally taken from Paul Thompson, *The Edwardians* (Paladin paperback 1977), to which the present book was first conceived as a photographic companion. The quotation with photograph 2.5 comes from an interview with a former Lancashire miner, Norman McEwan, by Gina Harkell; with 2.8, 3.16 and 7.7 from George Sims, *Living London*; with 6.15 from Annette Meakin, *Women in Transition*, 1907; with 7.10 from Elizabeth Chesser, *Woman, Marriage and Motherhood*, 1913.

We are grateful to the following for permission to use the photographs in this book:

Aberdeen City Library, for fig. 7.8

Beaford Archive, for fig. 4.15

Miss S. Bellamy, for fig. 4.11

Birmingham Reference Library, Sir Benjamin Stone Collection, for figs 1.4 and 1.5

Birmingham Reference Library, Local Studies Library, for figs 3.6 (Black Country Workers Collection), 3.20, 3.23, 3.24, 3.25, 3.27 and 3.28 (Bourneville Collection), 3.26 (Cadbury Collection), and 8.4

Bishopsgate Institute, for figs 5.7 and 5.8

Natasha Burchardt, for introduction fig. 3

Cambridgeshire Collection, Cambridgeshire Libraries, for figs 4.16, 8.5 and 8.10

David Cleveland and Messrs Colman of Norwich, for fig. 3.29

Country Life, for figs 1.3, 1.9, 1.10 and 7.16

Edinburgh City Libraries, for figs 4.5 (Grant Collection), 5.5 and 5.6

Edinburgh University, School of Scottish Studies, for fig. 5.2

George Ewart Evans and A. J. George, for fig. 3.9

Glasgow District Libraries (The Mitchell Library), for figs 3.13, 5.4, 6.11, 6.19 and 7.3

Greater London Council, for figs 1.7, 7.14, 8.1, 8.2, 8.3, 8.13

Hammersmith Central Library, for figs 5.11, 6.9 and 7.19

Hereford City Library, for fig. 3.8

High Wycombe Central Library for fig. 3.15 (from *High Wycombe as it was* by I. G. Sparkes)

W. Hillcourt and Lady Baden-Powell 8.9 (from *Baden-Powell*, Heinemann)

Kendal Public Library 4.2

Kodak Museum, for frontispiece and figs 1.8, 3.3, 3.4, 4.12, 6.1, 6.3, 6.5, 6.7, 6.8, 6.10, 6.13, 6.14, 6.20, 7.1, 7.2, 3, 4, 7.10, 7.15 and 7.18

Leeds Library for figs 3.21 and 7.4

Liverpool City Libraries, for figs 2.3 (by permission of the Director of Housing, Liverpool City Council), 2.6, 5.13, 9.8, 9.9, 9.10 and 9.11

London Transport, for fig. 3.18

Manchester Public Libraries, for figs 6.2, 6.4, 6.22, 8.14, 8.15 and 8.16

Manchester Polytechnic (Bill Williams), for figs 5.9 and 8.6

Mansell Collection, for figs 6.16, 7.11, 9.1 and 9.2

Evan Mead, for fig. 4.14

Frank Mullineux, for fig. 2.5

Museum of East Anglian Life, Stowmarket, for figs 4.13 and 6.21

Museum of English Rural Life, University of Reading, for figs 3.7, 3.8, 4.6 and 4.8

Museum of Lakeland Life and Industry, Abbot Hall, Kendal, for fig. 4.3

National Museum of Wales, for figs 3.1, 3.12 (photos by William E. Jones)

Dr Robert G. Neville, for figs 6.23, 9.6 (Mrs G. Bramley) and 9.7 (Keith Nield), all from *The Yorkshire Miners' In Camera* by Robert G. Neville (Nelson; Hendon Publishing, 1976)

Newcastle Central Library, for fig. 5.10

Northumberland County Record Office, for fig. 6.15

Nottinghamshire County Library, Local Studies Library, for fig. 7.17

Nottingham Historical Film Unit, for figs 3.22, 7.12 and 7.13

Radio Times Hulton Picture Library, for figs 1.2, 1.6, 3.11, 6.12, 6.17, 7.5, 7.6, 9.4, 9.5

E. Roe, for fig. 8.7

Royal Archive, Windsor (by Gracious Permission of Her Majesty The Queen), for fig. 1.11

Salford Local History Library and Cultural Services Department, Manchester, for fig. 3.14

Bill Eglon Shaw, The Sutcliffe Gallery, for figs 4.1 and 5.12

Sport & General, for fig. 1.1

South Shields Gazette, for fig. 7.9

Sir James Slater, Portsoy, for fig. 4.4

Strathclyde Regional Council, for figs 2.2 and 2.4 (from *Glasgow as it was* published by Hume and Moss)

Norris Thompson, for fig. 4.7

Victoria and Albert Museum, for fig. 5.1

Thea Vigne, for figs 3.19 and 6.6 (Frederic Brown) and 8.8 (Edwin Burden)

Wolverhampton Library, for figs 3.10 and 8.11

P. H. Youngman, for figs 4.9 and 4.10

Other Sources of Illustrations:

Batsford Collection: 3.17, 5.3

Paul N. Haseluck (ed), *The Book of Photography, Practical, Theoretical and Applied*, 1905, Introduction 1

Illustrated London News, 3 August 1912, 9.3

George Sims, *Living London*, 1902–3, 2.1, 2.7–11, 3.2, 3.5, 3.16, 7.7, 8.12

R. Mudie-Smith, *Sweated Industries*, 1906 exhibition catalogue, 3.7, 6.18

INTRODUCTION

The camera may not lie. But what kind of truth does it tell? Old photographs are deceptive. We look at them like snaps we might have taken ourselves: records of an instant moment from the past, which with the help of the photographic image, we can remember and reconstruct. Sometimes we can recall who those people were. Perhaps even what that day was like. But with an old photograph, in most cases, nobody knows who the people were. With luck, the place may be recorded, and less often, the date. It is possible to guess the date from clothing—although not very reliably, since some Victorian dress styles could be seen well into the twentieth century. More important, the picture has to be interpreted. What were the people doing, why were they in the picture, why was it taken? Photographs are silent, but we cannot rest with that: we need to see meaning in them. And where no message is given, we invent one. Most old photographs, therefore, are half pieces of history, half out of our own minds.

In another sense, however, photographs are never silent—even if no details of them are given. On the contrary, they suggest all sorts of meanings. For example, an Edwardian slum scene can evoke many different reactions—from criticism of the very existence of poverty, to suggestions that the poor were 'poor but happy' or, alternatively, 'incurable drunkards' who could have bettered themselves if they had worked harder. These various interpretations may all be latent in the photograph. But once a caption is added to it, this will immediately eliminate some possibilities, and direct the reader towards one meaning rather than another.

How closely need this message correspond with the feelings of the people in the photograph and the purposes of the original photographer? Photographs do not convey the consciousness of the people in them—why they were doing what they were doing, and what they felt about it. They were caught at a particular moment in time by someone with a camera who thought what they were doing was interesting. It might have been originally intended as a snap for a family album; or, by a newspaper editor, writer or official, to illustrate a particular pre-occupation or social problem. It is because most old photographs have been torn out of the context of meaning which could only be given by their subjects and those who took them, that it becomes possible for them to be re-interpreted in almost any plausible way that an author wishes to choose. In this book we have tried to direct the reader in one way rather than another with each photograph—and we believe you should be aware that we have done so. These photographs—like those in other books or newspapers—are meant to reconstruct our particular view of Edwardian Britain. Maybe you would interpret them differently: indeed, we suggest that you try.

Beyond this problem of interpretation there is another reason why photographs cannot be taken as straightforward mirrors of 'objective' reality. Photography from the very start has been an art as well as a technique. It took a long time to establish conventions of its own, independent of styles in painting. The earliest photographs of the mid-nineteenth century had to be taken in bright sunlight and carefully arranged for an exposure of more than five minutes. Their sharp black and white images precisely parallel the vivid exactness of the pre-Raphaelite painting of the 1850s. Later the fashionable painter's palate softened, and was echoed in exquisitely sensitive brown-tone studies of town and country, like those of Peter Emerson in East Anglia, and, from the late 1870s

Professional studio portraiture—complete with fake column.

onwards, Frank Sutcliffe of Whitby. Although technical improvements brought exposure time down to below one second by the 1870s, camera equipment remained cumbersome, and the typical picture was still highly self-conscious, posed after the photographer had set up his heavy dry plate apparatus on a tripod.

For the professional, this remained the principal method throughout the period, because it could ensure the highest technical standard. Informal work for press photography was only just beginning at this time. For studio photography, which remained the backbone of an ordinary professional's earnings, there was no practical alternative to the fixed pose. The flash, of magnesium powder or ribbon, was known before 1900, but scarcely used—one reason why there are so few informal photographs to show the insides of ordinary Edwardian homes, pubs or shops. Studio photographs froze the posed convention of earlier portrait painting, down to the baroque architectural detail or glimpse of landscape on the painted backdrop behind the sitter. It was also common for photographs, once taken, to be embellished with hand-painted colours. But the tight bond to the conventions of 'fine art' did not only affect the ordinary local commercial photographer. Its mark is equally clear at the other end of the profession, in the 'art photography' of the 1900s.

The British 'avant-garde' whose work was shown in international exhibitions and journals seemed determined to defy the essence of the photograph in muted tones and blurred outlines, water and city fog and smokescapes trailing behind the painting of the French Impressionists and Whistler's 'Nocturnes' of fully twenty years earlier. Inspiration from painting brought more inventive results in the work of art photographers from France and America: the first abstract photography—a decade after the Cubists—in A. L. Coburn's 'Vortographs', and the beginnings of the nude study. There were no such experiments by British photographers: indeed scarcely any openly sexual subject—even in full dress, like a town 'monkey parade'—seems to have been admissible for photography of any kind, and leaves the most gaping of all empty spaces in a camera account of the age.

Consequently, in the 1900s it is generally photographers with rather more conservative aesthetic attitudes who left the most worthwhile work. Sutcliffe has been mentioned; George Washington Wilson of Aberdeen, older still, is another. He set up a successful picture postcard firm, like Francis Frith of London and James Valentine of

Dundee. Wilson also took remarkable work and social scenes, but the mainstay of these firms was the village or town street view. These survive in immense numbers, and although the rural postcard often betrays the influence of 'rustic' imagery from painting, the town street is more often a straightforward record. There were fewer examples in painting to draw on, and although the people could be chosen and posed, the buildings at least were unalterable.

The same approach was also used for a new type of photograph which first became common in the 1900s—the documentation of slum areas deserving clearance, taken for council housing officials. Progressive councils like London, Glasgow and Liverpool took the fullest records. They also documented their work in education and health services. Their example was followed by just a few prison and workhouse authorities. These photographs are invariably posed, usually formally, and very often for a slum record the population of the dwellings has been called outside to stand by their doors. Officials were much less interested in the relatively healthy artisan districts or middle-class suburbs; nor were they as good a commercial proposition for postcards as main streets, so there tends to be a gap in the local record here.

For poverty, there was also another photographic tradition which can be traced back to the picturesque 'genre' paintings of low life by the seventeenth-century Dutch and Flemish painters. Gypsies, second-hand markets, barefoot urchins, street traders and tramps were already accepted subjects before 1900. With the growing social concern of the later nineteenth century, this type of photograph converged with the documentary, resulting in remarkable collections by pioneers of photographic journalism like the Chester press photographer Richard Eastham's 'Liverpool Views and Life Scenes', and George Sims' *Living London*.

In a similar way, there are ample camera records of types of work which were thought picturesque, like farm work, fisher girls or traditional crafts; while some photographs were also taken by social reformers of the worst 'sweated trades' as part of the minimum wage agitation for home workers. Another kind of work documentary was produced by a few progressive firms, especially in food manufacture, who were proud of their factory and office conditions. But this left out a whole series of major occupations. One can see why it was almost impossible to photograph men at work at sea, down a mine or on a railway engine; but there is also a noticeable absence of work pictures, for example, of domestic servants or steel workers. It is interesting that two of the most remarkable photographers of industrial working-class life shared that social background: William Graham of Glasgow, railwayman turned photographer after being sacked for his part in a strike, and William Jones of Abersychan, South Wales miner's son, whose pictures were taken for lantern slides to illustrate his father's socialist lectures.

Graham's most interesting photographs were taken in his spare time—like the East End ghetto pictures by another professional, C. A. Mathew of Brightlingsea in Essex. But by the 1900s the camera was no longer a costly luxury. The roll-film pocket Kodak had been introduced in 1895, followed by the Brownie in 1900 which cost only five shillings. Already the family and the leisure life of the upper classes was caught in private albums and in fashionable magazines such as *Country Life*, but now for the first time ordinary middle- and working-class family life began to be recorded. The new hand-held camera also made the genuinely informal 'snap' at last possible. The typical picture continued to be of posed well-scrubbed groups at weddings, picnics or the front door, although holiday photographs—especially on the beach, where the light was good—tended to break this pattern earlier. The first great master of informal photography was a London engraver, Paul Martin, whose street scenes and East Anglian beach snaps mostly date between 1890 and 1904, when he turned professional. In popularising the new approach the Kodak company itself played a key role. Leading photographers like Martin, and also Sutcliffe, were provided with the latest model cameras for experimentation, and selections of their work exhibited in London. Prizes were also offered to amateurs in annual photographic competitions. Both kinds of work survive in the Kodak Museum at Harrow, and the anonymous albums of competition entries form a particularly precious archive, a view of Edwardian family life as a whole which no other existing collection provides.

This, then, was the first decade of the ordinary amateur photographer. And that is why the pictures which have so far reached the archives can only be a foretaste of what might eventually be discovered. It will be all the more valuable if they can be collected along with the fullest possible detail about the people in them and their lives, which quite often can still be taken down from surviving subjects themselves. Some of the Sutcliffe portraits of fisherfolk, for example, have been quite recently identified and dated in response to newspaper appeals. In fact, there are rich possibilities for a new kind of local history which combines photographs with personal memories. Some of the photographs chosen here came to light incidentally through oral history work by Thea Vigne and Paul Thompson (others were printed in *The Edwardians*), or from a project at Manchester Polytechnic where local records, photographs and oral memories are collected hand in hand. The richness of photographic material to be discovered locally is vividly shown by booklets like those issued from the Nottingham Historical Film Unit; and another local booklet from North London, *The Changing Face of Newington Green*, published by The Factory (1977), suggests the added dimension of meaning to be gained from bringing together photographs with people's memories of the past. One hopes that much more local work of this kind will follow.

Our own concern here, however, is with national rather than local history. If photographs are such an uncertain and malleable kind of evidence as we have suggested, it may well be asked what value they have at all as a historical source. Statistics on birth rates, deaths, average wages and ownership of wealth are to a large extent indisputable. Autobiographies give us personal accounts of what life was like and put flesh on the bones of such general statistics. What role is there for the photograph? It is the ability of the photograph to show immediately the *physical* environment of the past which is its great boon to historical understanding. For example, we do not need to *imagine* with the help of written descriptions what the inside of a workhouse looked like at the turn of the century. With the photograph we are instantly there and can see for ourselves. The photograph may have been taken at a certain angle to emphasise certain features, but it is surely less approximate than a shady picture in our imagination. We can understand at a glance what prevailing attitudes towards the poor meant. Conversely, at the other end of the social

The slum photograph as a pictorial genre: three children of a Cardiff photographer pose as waifs in front of a fake wall painted on canvas. The bottom of the long dress, and the cigarette smoke have been painted in afterwards. The smoker is Maurice Edelman, later Labour MP and novelist. Taken c. 1915 by Joshua Edelman, who had emigrated from Poland twenty years earlier, and earned his living mostly from studio portraits, but also as a conjuror.

scale we can see how the rich dressed, their posture and demeanour, the restrictiveness of Edwardian dress for women, the elaborate materialism of a culture which believed that wealth, status and property ought to be openly paraded. Like the personal account, the photograph helps us to see the dimensions and inequalities of the wider social structure— such as can be statistically demonstrated with graphs of wealth and employment patterns and so on—in *human terms*; that is, through a kind of empathetic understanding, we can grasp what it was like to live then. Photographs, like first-hand accounts, can give us a sense of the past quite lacking in more conventional material. Those which follow have been chosen to set out, as far as the technical and conventional limits to camera use at the time permit, the main dimensions of Edwardian social life: the contrasts of leisure and work, riches and poverty, intimacy and tension.

SOCIETY

The Edwardian era was the Indian summer of the richest and most powerful ruling class the world had yet seen. Britain still just held the economic dominance she had won through leading the industrial revolution, even though America and Germany were edging up fast behind her. Through commerce, conquest and colonisation, one quarter of the world's surface flew the British flag. London was the world's financial and political capital. Yet this vast Empire was governed and owned by an extraordinarily small élite. In 1913 a mere 1% of the adult population of Britain owned more than two thirds of the national wealth—land, houses, stocks and shares, businesses and so on. Most of these owners were middle-aged or elderly men, for at that time such heads of families handed over much less to either wives or children before they died. Even those few of the very rich who had not been born with land and titles were usually set up with them by the end of their lives. Nine tenths of the land in Britain was landlord owned; and partly because of this the very biggest urban property-developers of the period, dock and railway and coal-owners, were generally aristocrats. The Edwardian aristocracy were also a governing class. They staffed the Army and Navy, provided the governors for the colonies and ambassadors to foreign powers. They dominated the cabinet and the Houses of Parliament. Even in the most Liberal House of Commons ever, elected in 1906, one sixth of MPs had been to Eton; and the House of Lords was still empowered to keep the Commons in line with its veto—until it overshot the mark by rejecting Lloyd George's 1909 budget.

This imperial aristocracy held their positions partly through commercial enterprise and political flexibility, and also through the military power they held in reserve. But equally important was the supreme self-confidence they instilled in themselves, and impressed on others, of their fitness to rule. Edwardian upper-class social life was designed to achieve this by fusing the sober duties of service to the community with theatrical and public displays of wealth and masculine strength. Banquets, church parades, naval and military reviews, durbars, hunts, cricket matches and races were all part of a great circulating social parade, impressing the governed and also seducing would-be opponents by sucking them into the social whirl. While Parliament was sitting, social life centred on the match-making drawing rooms and ballrooms of the capital; between sessions, it dispersed to the spas and resorts, the country houses and the grouse moors. Upper-class society was highly ritualised. Elaborate social etiquette was used to sniff out and eject intruders. Not that it was entirely exclusive. Connections were deliberately made with the City financial world, the intelligentsia and provincial leaders, so that London society was reflected at diminishing levels down the social scale in Oxbridge, the provinces and the Empire. But we focus on the top.

1.1 Fashions at Ascot: Edwardian ladies, with their rustling petticoats, tight lacing, and artificially wired-up hair to support their gorgeous hats, unable to dress without the help of a servant, were in themselves society's most luxurious objects of consumption. But they also managed the season: it was their business in life, while the men governed. An upstart was easy enough to spot, when each occasion required exactly the right dress and accessories. Ascot, for example, was the nearest to London that brown boots could be worn.

1.2 The aristocratic image: members of the Earl Fitzwilliam hunt taking wine from a tail-coated servant at Clumber, one of the Duke of Newcastle's three homes, in 1908. The vast house was pulled down thirty years later, but the lawns, the great trees and the three-mile avenue still mark the heart of the Duke's 35,000 acre domain; and at a discreet distance, the cottage estates which housed a respectful tenantry. Some village labourers might follow the hunt on foot.

1.3 Playing the game: the Eton Cricket Match against Harrow at Lords, 1900. The public boarding schools trained boys for the governing class. Team games, manly competition within accepted rules, provided a model for public life. The Lords match was also a fashion parade—and a family reunion.

1.4 Duties of the class: the House of Commons in Committee in 1906. Photographers were less often interested by such a sober company, dark-suited in dim rooms.

1.5 Outside, the river terrace of the Houses of Parliament affords another parade ground, while Richard Sadler, a Birmingham solicitor and Sutton Coldfield councillor, enjoys tea with strawberries. Both parliamentary pictures are by his host Sir Benjamin Stone, MP for Erdington.

1.6 Gentlemen at exercise: John Redmond and his wife riding in Hyde Park, July 1911. Rotten Row was a morning social display, as well as country exercise in the heart of the capital city. Redmond was leader of the Irish Nationalist MPs, with whose help the power of the Lords had just been broken; and his political demands challenged the unity of the Empire itself. But long years at Westminster had given him and his wife a social manner almost sufficient to match the sardonic smile from their companion.

1.7 Feasting: the New Vagabonds' Dinner for Hall Caine the novelist, chaired by the fashionable liberal Christian preacher R. J. Campbell, in the Grand Hall of the Hotel Cecil, London, December 1904. The Edwardian rich consumed huge quantities of food and drink: meat and fish four meals a day, with fresh fruit and vegetables from the estate, and plentiful cream, eggs, coffee, wines and spirits. A dinner for twenty people would cost about £60—more than the entire living expenses of a charwoman and her family for two years. Here the culturally aspiring London well-to-do follow their example.

1.8 Travelling officer: for this gentleman in summer uniform, surveying a Canadian railway timetable, a network of clubs offered seclusion, comfort and service in almost any town throughout the Empire. Clubs were exclusive common rooms for elected subscribers only; normally male preserves, like military messes and country house smoking rooms.

1.9 Sport: Lord Lonsdale at his butt on a shooting expedition, August 1910. Shooting had become the paramount sport for the wealthiest Edwardian aristocrats. Deer forests occupied three million acres in the Scottish north alone. Guests to the Duke of Westminster's Eaton Hall were expected to bring a thousand cartridges each. On the first day of a visit to Wynyards, the King's party shot 3000 rabbits. Lonsdale, with a reputed annual income of £2,000,000, Cumberland coal-owner as well as heir to an ancient estate, was also a boxer and motorist, first president of the AA. Known as the flamboyant Yellow Earl, he had a cavalcade of yellow carriages with liveried postilions, 84 hunting horses, a private orchestra, and a motor car of real silver. Lowther Castle is now a ruin.

1.10 A display of game shot in India, from *Country Life*, 1902. Baden-Powell prefaced *Scouting for Boys* by remarking how he progressed from catching and cooking rabbits as a schoolboy to 'endless fun big-game hunting in the jungles in India and Africa' in the Army. 'Then I got real scouting in South African campaigns.' The fun to be had from hunting was easily confused with that to be had from colonial wars.

I.II Before the war game became real: Queen Mary watches army manoeuvres in Northamptonshire, twelve months before the outbreak of the First World War. Even then, nobody imagined the endless slaughter of the trenches to come. War was expected to be over in a few weeks.

SECTION TWO

POVERTY

At the other end of the social scale was an economy of pinching, scraping, and want. The first urban poverty surveys at the turn of the century by Charles Booth in London and Seebohm Rowntree in York both found that more than a quarter of the city population had insufficient income to provide food and shelter for 'bare physical efficiency', let alone comfort. There was little room for waste in the economy of the slum. Children picked from rubbish heaps and gutters and under market stalls. They queued at public houses and restaurants for the day's leftovers. Their mothers bought broken biscuits and second-hand meat. When a London horse died, its parts were carefully divided for re-use: its skin was taken for leather, its bones boiled for oil and ground for manure, its flesh cooked for cat's meat, its footbone sent to the buttonmaker and its hoof to the glue factory. At refuse yards, women workers sorted rubbish for re-sale. With such cheap labour, recycling made good commercial sense.

In a wider sense, poverty did not just affect the poorest. The one million coal miners, for example, who hand-hacked out one of Edwardian Britain's principal exports, were already formidable trade unionists among the top manual wage-earners. But in most of the country they lived in squalid terrace rows without any indoor sanitation. When the Army called for recruits for the Boer War, it found that nearly two thirds of those who volunteered had to be rejected as unfit. Throughout the country, the middle and upper classes lived longer, grew taller than the working class. You were four times more likely to develop tuberculosis in central Birmingham than in well-to-do suburban Edgbaston. Expectation of life in middle-class Hampstead was fifty years at birth, in working-class Southwark thirty-six years. Behind these appalling figures lay not only low wages and unemployment, but unimproved slum environments in a Britain without health or welfare services.

The Edwardians did see the first tentative steps towards a welfare state. The Liberals conceded the school health service, and free meals for under-nourished schoolchildren, to Socialist pressure; and went on to introduce selective unemployment and health insurance schemes for workers, and a minimal pension for 'deserving' over-seventy-year-olds. But for most of those who fell on really hard times, especially women, children and the old, the only assistance still came from the Poor Law. Their last refuge remained the workhouse, the nearest link in that formidable chain of bastilles constructed after 1834 to terrify the poor into self-sufficiency.

2.1 Recycling in a subsistence economy: women workers, assisted by men with spades, sift rubbish at a London County Council depot. Dust was used for brick-making, china and hard core for roads, paper and soft core for manure, tins for ship ballast, glass for sandpaper, and so on. Women labourers earned under £30 a year.

2.2 Poverty of environment for top wage-earners: a characteristic miners' row at Templeton, near Glasgow, 1912. Note the unpaved street, open gutter and washtubs. With shift work, miners' women had to work round the clock providing food, baking, laundering, and washing their men in tin baths at the kitchen fire. There were no pithead baths yet. The typical row would have faced a fly-infested battery of communal earth closets, just to the left.

2.3 An inner city slum court off Silvester Street, Blenheim Street area, Liverpool; a documentary record for the city's housing officials in 1913. In Liverpool and London especially, the city councils for several decades had been slowly clearing the most ill-ventilated, over-crowded courts, but since council housing could only be built at unsubsidised rents well above the means of slum-dwellers, clearance simply drove the problem round the corner.

2.4 A Glasgow woman sitting in her bed recess: another official record taken around 1910. In Scotland half the housing stock consisted of one- or two-room dwellings—in the cities mostly tenements—and bed recesses commonly replaced separate bedrooms. For the sick or dying, for childbirth, for lovers, privacy was impossible. In the most over-crowded districts the Glasgow council 'ticketed' houses in an attempt to control numbers, subjecting families to night raids by inspectors with lanterns and notebooks. Council house-building had scarcely begun. Here was the cradle of Red Clydeside.

2.5 Manchester boys, around 1900. Slum boys got to know their cities well. They had to be out on the street because there was no space for them at home. By this age they would be truanting from school to pick up casual earnings for the family. Canals provided fun, and convenient free baths, especially close to warm water factory discharges. A Lancashire miner recalls: 'If you saw a pair of swimming shorts in the canals up there I bet St. Helens Corporation Baths was stamped on 'em—where they'd pinched 'em out the baths. You never saw the girls on the canal bank. Hundreds of lads. Nobody had any knickers on all the way down. There was no talk of nudism then. There'd be dead dogs in sacks and dead cats and you'd say, "The wind's blowin' that way, the ripples are goin' that way" '—you'd dive in. Anyone with a swimming costume he was well-off—rich. You never see any of that as kids.'

2.6 A charity feed: children outside the Food and Betterment Association Rooms, Lime Kiln Lane, Liverpool, photographed by Richard Eastham in 1904. Many families depended on charities for boots, blankets, second-hand clothes, and food in winter. Slum children were normally barefoot through the summer. Note the ill-fitting re-used clothes, the boys taking out bread, and the girl with a jug to carry home soup. One Salford slum boy, Richard Morgan, used to look forward to the Christmas breakfast which was the reward for a year's attendance at the Ragged School: 'We used to queue up at the morning and you went through the door a paper bag was given you and in this paper bag was a meat pie, a mince pie and a ham sandwich. And then you all sat down. . . . They serve you with tea. And then . . . you sang songs. . . . And as each child came out through the door they'd be given a present. A little girl gets a doll. A boy'd get a wooden fire engine or a wooden train. Everybody got something.'

2.7 Self-help by the homeless: squatters on Hackney Marshes. Every night, two thousand slept in the open on the central London streets. Others constructed makeshift shacks and tents on rubbish heaps and waste ground further out. The police moved them on, so that squatters' shanty towns, familiar in the colonies, never became part of the British urban scene.

2.8 A charity night's rest: at Medland Hall, Ratcliff, the London Congregationalist churches provided shelter and a piece of bread-and-butter for 450 homeless men nightly. Close to the docks, its clientele was of all nationalities, and ranged from the young farm labourer who could have 'stepped straight out of Mr Thomas Hardy's pages' to 'an unshorn outcast in a faded, rusty frock coat, unmistakeably a clerk, one of the City's rejected'. The bunks had seaweed mattresses and artificial leather sheets, disinfectable but non-porous; experienced dossers brought old newspapers for linings to absorb sweat.

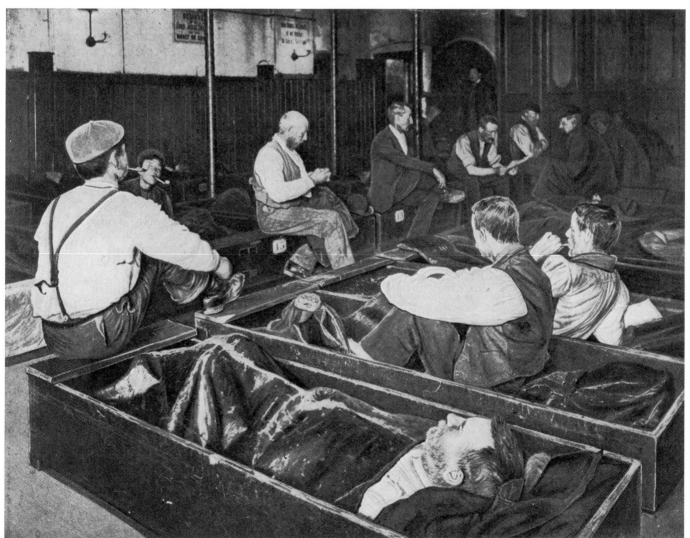

2.9 Flitting: a commoner method of getting cheap shelter was to move from house to house defaulting on the rent. Alice Towey from the Potteries lived in eight or more houses in five years. 'They wouldn't pay the rent . . . there was empty houses, hundreds of them. That's all you've got to do, go and give 'em sixpence for a key. . . . So when they'd been in so long and they didn't pay the rent—they got made to pay the rent. We never dared have a fire on the Mondays when the landlord was round. We didn't. No. Cos he never knew which house we were in.' In London, there were even firms specialising in moonlit flits. This move in 'Slumopolis', from George Sims' *Living London* of 1901, is not at the lowest level; the family has a table and chair, and a clock.

2.10 and 2.11 The Marylebone Workhouse, London in 1901: casual poor waiting for admission, and the dining room within. By the age of seventy, one Edwardian in five was a pauper, and by seventy-five, almost one in three. The broth and dumpling diet was better than many had at home, but the old, since they were not given false teeth, could hardly eat it. This institution housed two thousand men, women and children. George Lansbury, East London socialist, recalled the shock of his first visit to the workhouse as a Poplar Guardian: 'It was not necessary to write up the words "Abandon hope all ye who enter here". Officials, receiving ward, hard forms, whitewashed walls, keys dangling at the waist of those who spoke to you, huge books for name, history, etc., searching, and then being stripped and bathed in a communal tub [to be reclothed in coarse, ill-fitting uniform dress]—everything possible was done to inflict mental and moral degradation.'

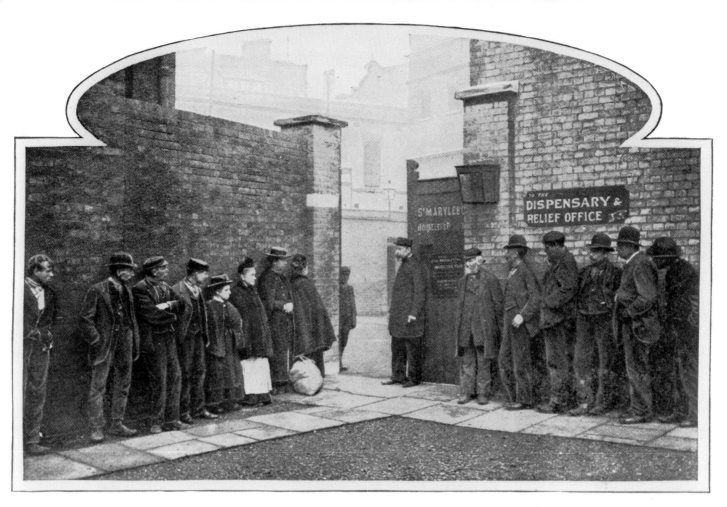

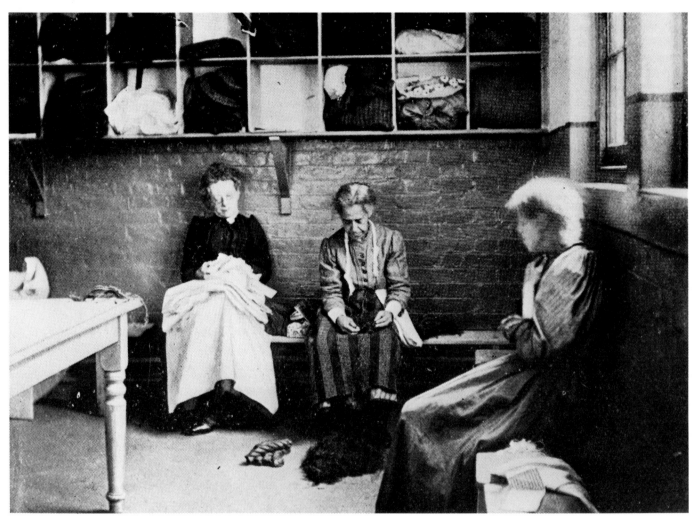

2.12 The Labour Test: women picking oakum in a casual ward, 1906. Able-bodied adults had to carry out task work in return for a night's shelter—men, for example, did a morning's stone-breaking. The social effects of slumps and low wages were scarcely understood except by the minority of socialist militants: even the Fabians believed the hard core of the very poor were degenerate 'loafers'. Tract 126 in 1906 recommended that these idlers who had 'never done a fair share of work and never will' should be treated under the criminal law. 'The weak minded and incompetent must be dealt with in farm colonies. . . . The deliberately idle must be set to hard labour, and their social vice, if it may be, sweated out of them.' Ironically, the First World War brought a quicker solution, and emptied the casual wards by bringing full employment for the first time.

SECTION THREE

WORK

Those who could not work, and those who had no need to, made the bottom and top of the social ladder. In between lay the great Edwardian majority, for whom constant work alone could keep their families above the poverty line, bring home the daily sub, the weekly wage packet or the monthly salary. At this time work in most places was scarce, for the normal national unemployment rate fluctuated around 10%. In this situation men were literally willing to fight for work. And women were prepared to migrate right across the country to earn less than a living wage—for the *average* Edwardian woman's annual pay was just £50, scarcely half than that of an average man, and below that of an unskilled labourer.

The very cheapness of labour made for a wasteful use of the workforce. The largest single occupation was still domestic service: one third of all women workers were servants. It was still cheaper for middle-class families to employ maids than to buy labour-saving equipment. Married women generally spent most of their time on the same tasks unpaid, for—except in the Lancashire cotton towns and a few other places—they did not normally go out to work. Some did part-time home manufacturing, probably the worst-paid work of all. In these 'sweated' home industries cheap labour was an alternative to mechanisation, and low wages generally probably explain why British businessmen had been so much slower than Americans in introducing (often British) technological advances. The average American industrial worker was already assisted by twice as much horse-power as the British, and this was the key reason why American living standards were to go ahead so much faster in the twentieth century.

All the same, this was a period in which the character of work and the way in which it was divided between the sexes were changing fast. For girls, the advent of the typewriter, the telephone and the multiple store provided new alternatives to service or factory work, edging out the male shop assistant and clerk. For men, the special satisfactions of craft skills and the workshop community, or the simple pride in manual strength, were gradually being ousted by factory production. Electrical power and lighting were spreading in factories. So was a more subtle approach to management, in which trade unionism was recognised, and amenities like canteens were provided. The Quaker chocolate manufacturers, Cadbury in Birmingham and Rowntree (of the social survey) in York, set the model for a future in which welfare provision, and humane consideration at work, was to soften the harshness of Edwardian class inequality. But they stood out as exceptions. For most Edwardians work was strenuous, in poor conditions; and for many it was dangerous. The working week lasted 55 hours or more. Still more than now, it dominated their lives.

3.1 South Welsh pitwomen queuing for pay, 1905. The office was a better place for distributing pay than the pub, the commonest alternative. Women labourers earned under £30 a year, about the same as charwomen; miners £100; a High Court judge £5000. This picture was used as a lantern slide for trade union and socialist lectures by Jabez Jones.

3.2 'Eager for work': gangers at the London docks pick out casual labourers for work. There were a third more dockers than could get work on an average day, and with several 'calls' daily many spent much of the week waiting. Penned like cattle behind the chain, they would not uncommonly fight for the last work tickets at a 'call'.

3.3 Fishergirls gutting herring, a Kodak snapshot of the early 1900s by Frank Sutcliffe of Whitby. The ship's funnel probably belongs to one of the newly introduced steam drifters, which were replacing herring sailboats. Every autumn some 5000 Scots herring girls, many from the outer islands, followed the boats down the east coast to Yarmouth.

3.4 LEFT   In service: one third of all women workers were domestic servants, living in their employers' households: cooking, carrying up coal and hot water, and caring for their employers' children. Usually they ate apart and slept in the attic. Devices such as vacuum cleaners and central heating had been invented, but were not yet economic. Photographs of servants at work are rare: this is a Kodak competition entry of 1912.

3.5   Better-off working-class households as well as town middle-class families paid to have their front steps washed. Although this was cold work in winter, step-girls, according to *Living London*, enjoyed a 'liberty' soon lost by 'the hard-driven sisterhood of more mature years who offer their services as charwomen'.

3.6 Metal craftswoman: a Cradley Heath chainmaker at work in the lean-to forge attached to her home, watched by her child. Low pay allowed independent craft work to survive in Midland metal trades long after American competitors had mechanised.

3.7 Toymaking: an unmechanised craft carried on as a home industry, chiefly by married women. In such 'sweated industries', despite working long hours into the night and being helped by children from an early age, a woman could commonly earn little more than five shillings a week.

3.8 A craft élite still unchallenged by machinery: a Herefordshire cooper's workshop of c. 1915. On the right, a stave is being hollowed on a shaving horse; on the left, a band is being riveted. Proud of their skills, the cooper's workshop community maintained traditional work standards as well as drinking customs and social etiquette. Note the hats, waistcoats and ties. Customary greeting was 'Morning Gentlemen all!'

3.9 A Norwich 'Snob': an old-fashioned independent cobbler, Mr Rix of Pottergate, at work on his last in his own work-room. Shoes were still put together by Norwich out-workers, but soon their main trade would be in mending rather than making boots and shoes.

3.10 Mass-produced boots and shoes: Craddock's factory, Wolverhampton. The boot trade fought off American imports through rapid mechanisation in the 1900s. A boy worker stands behind the overlooker in coat and cap.

3.11 Cathedral of labour: John Brown's shipyard, Clydeside. Shipbuilding was a craft operation on a Gargantuan scale, carried out by the highly paid, tightly unionised boilermakers, labour aristocrats of the industrial revolution. British yards were still producing over half the world's new ships in 1914, and 90% of the world's tramp steamers belonged to Britain.

3.12 South Welsh hewer, photographed by William Jones. Coal, another growth export, was still almost entirely hand-cut and—unlike in America—coal-cutting machines were little used. Miners were responsible for their own equipment; accidents were frequent. At the Senghynedd explosion in 1913, 439 men were killed. For the miner, having the strength and courage to work in the pit was a part of becoming a man.

3.13 Foundrymen: Kerr, the oldest blacksmith, and Alex Marshall, hammerman, in the North British Railway works at Cowlairs, c. 1900. Machine-making, engine-building and railway carriage production were important export industries based again on skilled labour. This rare picture of an old industrial worker is by William Graham, who turned photographer after being sacked by the railway for striking in 1891.

3.14 Barrels being hand-stacked with aid of pulleys in a Trafford Park warehouse, Manchester. At the top a barrel is being tapped for inspection—and perhaps a free drink all round. One of an unusual series of pictures whose photographer had a futurist eye for industrial geometry.

3.15 Navvies: some of the last of the great army of migrant labourers who built the Victorian railway system, at work in 1905 widening the Chiltern ridge cutting beyond High Wycombe for the new London Marylebone–Birmingham route.

3.16 Excavating the London underground: work on the Northern Line in 1903. Navvies digging with pickaxe and spade are backed by the great circular cutting edge of the metal shield, powered by hydraulic jacks. The deep tubes were a social as well as technical breakthrough: single-class electric trains in which the office boys could sit 'in great content beside the City magnate, and still the heavens do not fall!'

3.17 and 3.18 Transport revolution: a London tramway horse stables at Mare Street, Hackney, in 1902, and Cricklewood motor bus garage in 1906. The first London electric tramway opened in 1901, the first successful motor bus services in 1905. Once started, the ousting of the horse was especially rapid in public transport. As the photographs suggest, the new technology was at first fitted into traditional work discipline. At this time railwaymen too were known to their employers as 'railway servants'; and on the roads, the typical driver was in private service. The motor would change all that.

3.19 and 3.20 The typewriter girl and the boss: the Manager's Office of the motor accessory purchasing section of Brown Brothers Limited, Birmingham, cycle and motor part suppliers and manufacturers, c. 1910. Cycle-making was one of Britain's most advanced industries, and the office telephones and typewriter were progressive innovations at this date. The typewriter introduced a new clerical role for women as secretaries: servicing the male boss at work as an alternative to domestic service in the home. In the long run it meant the end of the typical Edwardian clerical workers, still men, writing by hand, seen in the General Office of Cadbury's in 1912—and the establishment of one of the most striking sexual divisions of labour today.

3.21 Factory production: women weavers at Glover Brothers' Wortley Low Mills, Leeds, West Yorkshire. The Pennine textile mills had been the spearhead of the British industrial revolution, and although now an old industry, remained prosperous: half of Britain's exports were in textiles and Britain still dominated the world cotton trade. Girls and young women made up most of the textile workforce and weavers were their largest skilled grade. Mill work was noisy and hot and the exposed machinery and steam power belts were dangerous, occasionally catching a girl's hair and scalping her.

3.22 Lacemakers: mending lace broken during manufacture at T. I. Birkin and Company's lace factory, Basford, Nottingham in 1914. Abundant lace was required for Edwardian fashions in dress, curtains, table cloths and so on. The mill is a typical early industrial structure with a framework of cast-iron pillars and joists within a brick shell.

3.23 Food factory: the marzipan room at Cadbury's, Bourneville, c. 1900. Mass production here depends on highly organised hand labour. The white dress underlines the need for hygiene.

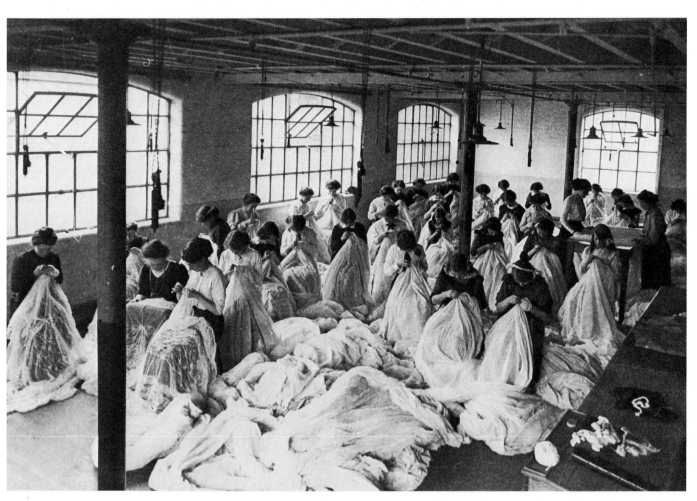

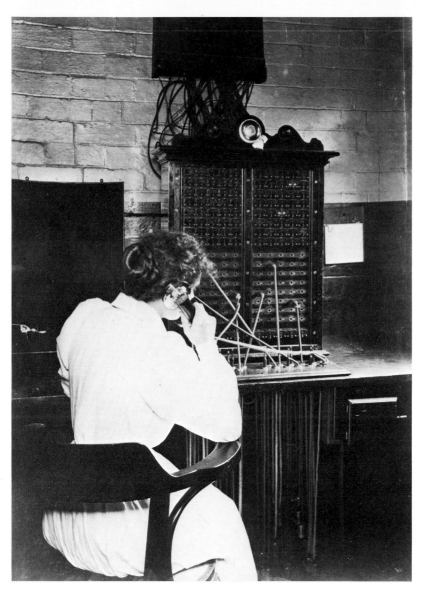

3.24 Cadbury's telephonist, 1905: another new white collar service job for women. In private homes the telephone, like the door, was answered by servants.

3.25 BELOW Progressive tableau: women workers in the dinner hour at the Bourneville Works lily pond, c. 1900. For the publicity photograph, two girls have been encouraged to cross the normally forbidden grass. George Cadbury's factory canteens, welfare rooms, gardens and leafy model cottage suburb for his workers were far ahead of their time.

3.26 and 3.27 RIGHT The Bourneville canteens for women and for clerks. The mixing of the sexes at work was regarded as morally dangerous. Nor was factory welfare intended to challenge the factory heirarchy. The male clerks have table plants, napkins, and women servants.

3.28 and 3.29 At the work gates: dinner breaks. The Cadbury's office staff enter under an arts and crafts rose trellis. Men from Colman's big food factory close to the centre of Norwich walk home into the city. Note the variety of headgear: the cloth cap is not yet an emblem of the manual working class.

SECTION FOUR

COUNTRYSIDE

Edwardian Britain was the most urban nation in the world. The village community had been drained to work the industrial revolution. Three quarters of its people lived in towns and cities, and a mere 7% of its workforce was still in agriculture. By 1900 the great wave of migration to the factories was over, and the countryside lay in a lull of quiet decay. The motor car had not yet broken its peace to make the high-hedged lanes the playground of the towns. It was a land of poetic beauty. But farmers, unaided by state subsidies or protective tariffs, could scratch little more than a bare living. Four fifths of Britain's wheat was shipped in from abroad. The splendour of the country houses rested no longer on returns from the land, but on infusions of new industrial wealth. Farm labourers were the lowest-paid large group of working men.

The countryside divided into two very different regions. In southern and eastern England, and parts of eastern Scotland, arable corn-farming predominated, and the tenant farmers who leased the land from the local county landowners worked it with the help of a large class of landless labourers. It was a society of still quite populous villages, and sharp inequalities. Western and northern Britain, by contrast, was pastoral, and more egalitarian. It was mostly sheep and cattle hill country worked in scattered farms by family labour, with the few hired men living in with the household. And at its furthermost fringe, the northern and western Scottish coast and islands, were clusters of crofting communities, townships of smallholders with small arable plots of their own, and large common grazings. Many townships were over-populated and during these years land-hungry crofters seized and took over a series of large tenant farms to set up new townships. In contrast to the south-east, here there were few great country houses, and landowners were mostly absentees, with insufficient social influence to curb endemic rebelliousness.

4.1 Family hill farm: women feeding the hens at Stainton Hall Farm, Danby, North Yorkshire. Farm buildings of local stone and pantiles, with a dry-stone wall behind the haystack. The stack has been cut back from its circular stone base to the beautiful sculptural shape which caught Frank Sutcliffe's eye.

4.2 Hiring day for farm workers in Kendal. In the north and west most farm-hands lived in, and were 'hired' for the year or half-year at local fairs. They stroll up and down, waiting to strike a bargain with a farmer. The stand shows pictures of the Boer War.

4.3 Sheep country: on the Cumbrian fells, near Kendal.

4·4 The bothy system: in north-east Scotland the arable farms needed more labour, so the unmarried hands were fed from the farmhouse kitchen, but slept in outbuildings like the barn lofts. Bad farm cooking would be pilloried in bothy ballads sung at the next hiring fair.

4·5 Planting potatoes in the Highlands. The man is digging with a foot plough or 'caschrom'; on the ground is a handwoven basket carried on the back by the woman. Women were the labourers in the crofting communities. The land may have been too rough for a horse plough; nor would there have been the cash to keep a horse here. In the islands the economy was so close to subsistence that eggs were used for currency, and the typical home was still a leaking thatched 'black house', often without windows or chimney, shared with the cattle.

4·6 Corn country in the south: ploughing with an early motor tractor. The mature trees suggest a country house estate. Large landowners had the resources to pioneer agricultural mechanisation. The picture comes from a slide collection used at the Writtle Institute of Agriculture in Essex.

4.7 Turning at the end of a furrow: a postcard sent from Lincolnshire in 1913. Even in the south, the horse still dominated farm work into the 1930s. Horsemen had to be strong—and skilled: 'it is so difficult especially to keep a straight line', reads the card.

4.8 Harvesting oats: a southern scene. Mechanical mowing had replaced hand reaping, but the corn was still sheafed, bound and stooked by hand. Women, who had largely dropped out of full-time farm work in the south, were still needed for the harvest. From a postcard sent from Wales, c. 1903.

4.9 and 4.10 Stacking and thrashing the East Anglian harvest at Charsfield, Suffolk. In the first photograph the superb horse-drawn wagon is obscured by its own load, but it can be glimpsed in the second: notice also the hand-made hurdles, and the great thatched barns. Thrashing tackle, normally worked through the winter by travelling contract teams, was the only power-driven machinery in general use for Edwardian farm work.

4.11 PREVIOUS PAGE Farmer and men: bowler-hatted, bow-tied Mr Barton watches his shearers at work at Hackwood Farm, Basingstoke, Hampshire, c. 1900. Big southern farmers aspired to be gentry, rather than manual workers. But not all survived the agricultural depression: as the old verse went:—

> *Man to the plough, Wife to the cow,*
> *Girl to the yarn, Boy to the barn,*
> *And your rent will be netted:*
> *Man Tally-ho! Miss piano,*
> *Wife silk and satin, Boy Greek and Latin,*
> *And you'll all be gazetted.*

4.12 BELOW Rural poverty: a Kodak competition photograph of c. 1910. Poaching was ubiquitous, irrepressible in the countryside: hunger still drove labourers to hunt for their own food.

4.13 Village craftsman: the general smithy at Grundisburgh, Suffolk. Migration to the towns undercut the independent tradesmen, but the larger villages could support a builder, wheelwright and blacksmith.

4.14 Poultry farmer: Isaac Mead and his two sons boxing turkeys for the London market in 1909. Smallholdings provided a chance for labourers to work their way up, but in Britain there was still little specialised poultry farming apart from the Heathfield smallholders in Sussex. Mead began turkey-rearing at Waples Mill, Margaret Roding, Essex, in 1903.

4.15 Social centre: Mrs Callard in her shop at Ashreigney, north Devon. Biscuits, chocolates, tea and sugar were mostly weighed out by hand, allowing plenty of time for conversation. However, in the midst of agricultural production, farm wages were too low for most labourers to afford fresh meat or milk, which were often difficult to buy, and more expensive than in the towns. Clothes were home-made, or bought from packmen who toured the countryside on foot.

4.16 Pump and water cart by the river Lark at Prickwillow in the Cambridgeshire Fens. Few English villages had piped water, electricity or sewers before the 1930s. Water had to be fetched from pumps, wells, ponds or streams. Prickwillow itself was a drained marsh parish mostly below sea level, rich farmland kept dry by giant steam pumping engines.

SECTION FIVE

CITY AND TOWN

The early twentieth-century urban scene was astonishingly diverse. At one extreme was the sleepy market town, imbedded in the countryside. But most Edwardians lived in small towns, from which they could walk straight out into the fields. Some were commercial centres, others industrial, normally concentrating on a single type of industry which gave them a distinctive atmosphere. In the textile, pottery and boot-making towns both men and women worked in the factories. In the iron and steel and coal communities, on the other hand, there was only tough, high-paid work for men. Garrison towns and ports were different again, rowdy and rough, ministering to sailors and soldiers with pubs and brothels. Seaside and inland spa towns, by contrast, and similarly Oxford and Cambridge, were dominated by the middle classes, respectable and genteel.

At the other extreme was London with its seven million people, the world's largest city, cosmopolitan as an international seaport, pattern for the conurbations of the future. Its central thriving hub of commerce and fashion was surrounded by a decaying inner ring of poorer districts, across which came a daily wave of bus, tram and train commuters housed in the healthier outer suburbs. In the old city, rich and poor had lived intermingled; transport now allowed sharply differentiated residential neighbourhoods, ranging from the well-to-do suburb to the immigrant ghetto. Manchester, Liverpool, Birmingham and Glasgow were also big cities of over a million, whose commercial and industrial magnates had similarly distanced their families from the hazards of the inner slums.

Housing standards varied strikingly, not just between the classes but also between regions. In southern English towns, apart from London, most houses had six or more rooms with running water and usually gas laid on, and increasingly often a bathroom too; but in the northern industrial towns the typical home was a two-up two-down house with a lavatory out in the backyard. In west Yorkshire the back-to-back was the standard type, and still being built. Roughly one quarter of these houses had no drainage, so that excrement from privies had to be shovelled out at intervals into barrows by sanitary gangs. Birmingham alone had 40,000 houses without either drainage or a water tap. But crowding was still worse in Scotland, where half the dwellings had only one or two rooms. And everywhere the worst slums were not the Victorian terraces which have been condemned since, but much older stock which had survived in the hearts of most towns from a pre-industrial era. Some slum clearance had begun, but little rehousing. This was the environment in which an infant born in the primitive economy of the three Scottish crofting counties had twice as good a chance of surviving its first year as an average English child: three times as good as in the Lancashire cotton towns, the potteries, or many Durham mining settlements; five times as good as a workhouse child from London.

5.1 World metropolis: the congested traffic of the imperial capital. Horse traffic at St Giles' Circus, London, c. 1900. Buses for Gospel Oak and London Bridge; in the background, a brewery, an elegant shopfront and commercial hoardings. Redevelopment is in progress at one corner; papers for sale at the other.

5.2 Slumber: barefoot children watch a herd of goats in the Market Square of Melrose on the Scottish Borders, c. 1900. There is a confectionery shop, a pub, and the Station Hotel, but as yet, no road traffic.

5.3 Salubrity: Lord Street, Southport, on the Lancashire coast in 1912. Southport began as a fashionable bathing resort in the early nineteenth century, but by this date was also a middle-class suburban town for the cotton towns and Liverpool. Late nineteenth-century iron verandahs shelter the shops and Rowntree's Café—tea-rooms were an important new town facility, providing a respectable meeting place for ladies. The spire of Christ Church, built in 1862, was given by a Preston cotton manufacturer.

5.4 Industrial city: view from a Glasgow tenement, taken by William Graham. Railway sidings, factory chimneys, smoke, hoardings advertising Pear's soap, and a woman hanging out her washing; on the right some of the tenement children, including a baby in a shawl.

5.5 Edinburgh fishing families: New Lane, Newhaven, with boats beached at the end of the street, c. 1905. There are separate dwellings on each floor, entered from up or underneath the stone stairs. Inshore fishing was a family concern: women baited the lines and helped mend the nets at home, and hawked the catch round the city. Fishing communities kept an independent culture, even within the city: note the Victorian bonnets, shawls and striped skirts, little changed since the earliest pictures by the pioneer Scots photographer David Octavius Hill in the 1840s.

5.6 The Royal Mile, Edinburgh: former fashionable homes of the Scottish aristocracy in Canongate had become sub-divided tenements in the poorest ward of the city. In a healthy middle-class suburb, ninety-six infants out of a hundred would survive their first year of life; in a slum like this, one in every three would be dead.

5.7 4% philanthropy: artisan dwellings built by trusts, which had to bring a modest profit on investment, were commoner than council housing, even on slum clearance sites. Very high densities ensured a rent which the better-off working class could afford. The City of London Artizans Dwellings here stand between Petticoat Lane and the underground Circle Line, cut behind the poster-plastered wall which advertises local entertainments: boxing at Premierland, and *A Girl's Temptation*, a melodrama at the Pavilion Theatre, Whitechapel Road.

5.8 Children of the London ghetto: Crispin Street, Whitechapel, on an April Saturday in 1912, taken like the previous picture by a strolling photographer from the Essex yachting town of Brightlingsea, who was probably waiting for a train at Liverpool Street. The children, who followed him round, included some in their best dress whom he had picked up outside the Sandys Row synagogue. The Jewish immigrants to the East End had been preceded by the French Huguenots and the Irish; today, their Great Synagogue is a Benghali Mosque.

5.9 Tailoring sweatshop and second-hand clothes dealer in Great Jackson Street, Hulme, Manchester. Jewish immigrants took up the cheap clothing trades of the inner city areas, succeeding through long hours and a highly organised division of family hand labour. The proprietor here was Samuel Smolensky, whose father Isaac, a Roumanian immigrant tailor of the 1880s, had given evidence to the Lords Committee on Sweating.

5.10 RIGHT Open street markets afforded the best value for the city poor: Newcastle women inspecting second-hand clothes at Paddy's Market, c. 1900.

5.11 Suburban shopping: Palmer's big provision store in Hammersmith, 1902. Note the displays of meat and daringly piled up tins. Before the 1911 Shops Act reduced hours, evening opening was common and assistants worked an average of over 70 hours weekly. Individual service was at the price of lengthy queues, especially late on Saturday night when meat prices were cut, and clerical workers too were ready to join the hunt for bargains.

72

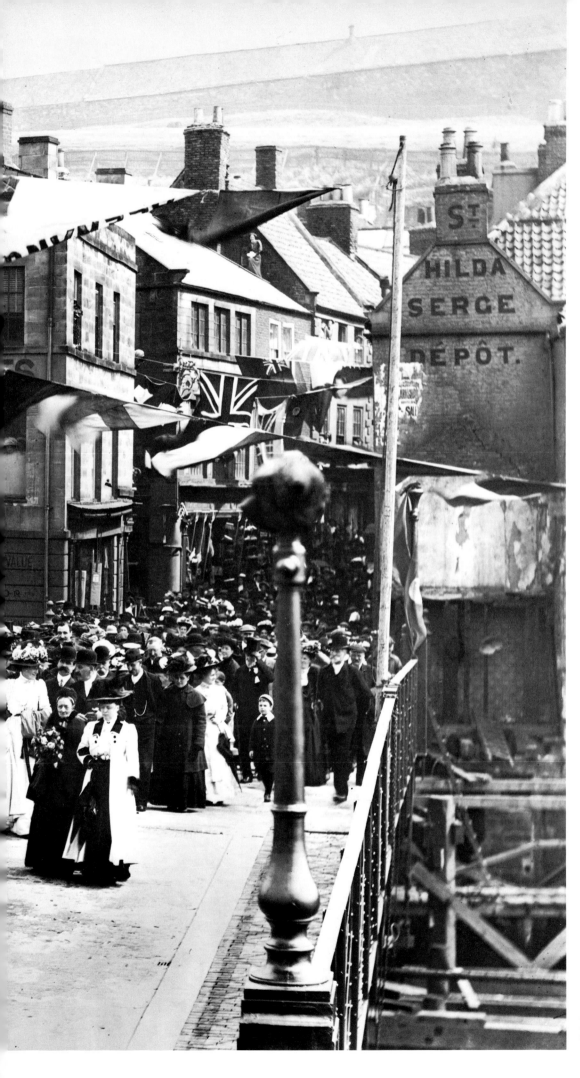

5.12 Civic dignity: Mrs Gervais Becket opens the swing bridge at Whitby, on 21 July 1908. Note the old church on the skyline, the cash drapery stores, and the photographer perched on the butcher's roof.

5.13 City culture: the grand St George's Hall, built for meetings and concerts, can just be seen behind Liverpool's monument to Wellington. Less attention was given to amenities for the out-of-work. Photographed in 1901 by Richard Eastham, then a struggling freelancer. Before being accepted for *To-day*, his first collection of street scenes was rejected by nine periodicals.

THE CYCLE OF LIFE

Life for an Edwardian was shorter than today: on average, under fifty years. Infancy especially was more dangerous. It was not until the first decade of this century that infant mortality in the towns began to fall. This was due partly to improved sanitation, partly to a new emphasis on health clinics, germ-free milk, and breastfeeding.

The authority of Edwardian parents, and particularly of the father as head of the household, was accepted with less question than today. Children were expected to respect their elders, and most of them did. In ordinary families many of them were emotionally close to their parents too. But there were exceptions. In those better-off families whose children were handed over to servants to be brought up in the nursery, and then sent off to boarding school, there was inevitably a much greater distance between parents and children than would be common in equivalent homes today. At the other end of the social scale, by contrast, children were forced by poverty into early independence. They had to play in the street because there was not enough room for them in the home; and long before they left school, they had to learn to pick up a living from charity, odd jobs, street selling and foraging.

Most girls and boys started work as soon as they left school at fourteen, at first in menial, low-paid jobs. The chance of apprenticeship, or the strength needed for adult labouring, did not come for a year or so. Puberty was also at that time normally after leaving school, courting beginning perhaps at sixteen, and marriage delayed to an average age of 26. Yet despite this long wait, Edwardians showed patient restraint. Illegitimacy was rare, and in decline; and this could not yet be explained by the spreading use of contraceptives. The same is true of the shrinking number of children born after marriage. The aristocracy had already started the rebellion against Victorian inhibition. But for others, sexual passion was curbed, probably more than it had ever been.

Marriage was the expected social fulfilment for women, and to the better-off it brought an improved social standing. But with servants already less easy to find, wives may well have been more confined to housework than at any other time. In all classes most women gave up work: more, in fact, than ever before. For ordinary working-class families, especially if a succession of children needed to be fed, this brought a period of struggle on the poverty line. Then, as the first children began to earn, things would improve for a while. The burden of this struggle fell most heavily on the mother, for the man, as breadwinner, had to be kept fit. It was a man's world, so long as his strength lasted. There were fewer old people then. They survived in the fear of the workhouse; but most had the better fortune to be taken in for their last years by their children or grandchildren.

6.1 Mother and child: this rare photograph of informal infancy by Frank Sutcliffe reflects the new Edwardian concern for motherhood and infant welfare and anticipates the close bonding which by the 1930s was to be the ideal of middle-class motherhood.

6.2 Infant orphans at Crumpsall Workhouse, Manchester. In the age before safe substitutes for breastfeeding had been discovered, these babies were the most vulnerable of all.

6.3 and 6.4   See-saws: a Kodak competition
family entry, and Crumpsall Workhouse children—
boys, shorn, but still not allowed to wear trousers.
Boys in all classes still commonly wore skirts and
long hair as infants.

6.5 Learning to be a woman: another Kodak entry, of 1904.

6.6 Learning to be men: family business heirs, grandchildren of Frederic Brown senior, founder of Brown Brothers, the Birmingham motor manufacturers, photographed in 1904.

6.7 Fun for boys in Trafalgar Square, c. 1912. Photographs of naked urchin swimmers had been made fashionable by Sutcliffe's Whitby 'Water Rats' of 1886, which Edward VII himself, then Prince of Wales, had enlarged to hang in Marlborough House, despite objections to the picture from the clergy. Boys—but not girls—could earn a penny by stripping off and posing for the photographer: in this instance, a Kodak competitor.

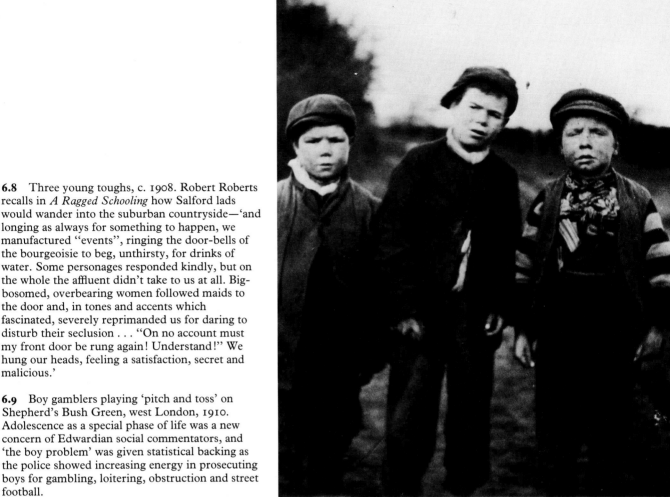

6.8 Three young toughs, c. 1908. Robert Roberts recalls in *A Ragged Schooling* how Salford lads would wander into the suburban countryside—'and longing as always for something to happen, we manufactured "events", ringing the door-bells of the bourgeoisie to beg, unthirsty, for drinks of water. Some personages responded kindly, but on the whole the affluent didn't take to us at all. Big-bosomed, overbearing women followed maids to the door and, in tones and accents which fascinated, severely reprimanded us for daring to disturb their seclusion . . . "On no account must my front door be rung again! Understand!" We hung our heads, feeling a satisfaction, secret and malicious.'

6.9 Boy gamblers playing 'pitch and toss' on Shepherd's Bush Green, west London, 1910. Adolescence as a special phase of life was a new concern of Edwardian social commentators, and 'the boy problem' was given statistical backing as the police showed increasing energy in prosecuting boys for gambling, loitering, obstruction and street football.

6.10 A street corner playground outside a park, probably in south London, with a food stall in the background. In poor families boys as well as girls had to help look after younger children. Taken just before 1900 by Paul Martin, the first professional master of the informal snapshot, experimenting with a Kodak camera.

6.12 Couple on a Bank Holiday in the Midlands, c. 1904. Edwardian photographers lacked the interest—or courage—to snap a 'monkey parade', or a working-class lad in his pointed clogs and brass-buckled belt with his jockey-capped, waistcoated, cigarette-smoking girl.

6.13 Self-scrutiny. With marriage her best social chance, a young girl was concerned with her physical appearance from an early age. A Kodak competition entry of c. 1908.

6.14 Suppressed sexuality: another Kodak photographer of c. 1904 festoons his pre-pubescent girl subject alluringly. Did he know that her pose could be traced back to erotic eighteenth-century French paintings by François Boucher? Could this be by J. B. B. Wellington, first manager of the Kodak Harrow works in the 1890s, later to exhibit an art photograph of similarly 'innocent' naked girlhood entitled 'Mother's Jewels'? In Britain—unlike France and America—adult women were not yet an accepted subject for the nude study, even in art photography: this was as close as the Edwardian dared to peep.

6.15 The wedding day of Brenda Bertram in Northumberland, 11 August 1909. 'If there is anything quite certain it is that the normal destiny of a woman is to be a mother, and that any woman, however otherwise successful, who has not achieved this station, has essentially failed', wrote Annette Meakin two years earlier.

6.16 Paterfamilias of a well-to-do family checks his daughter's musical progress. In families with servants to relieve them of housework, music, embroidery and watercolour painting were among the few home activities permitted as alternatives to entertaining guests.

6.17 Family tea, c. 1910. There is no servant here, and the strain of keeping up appearances on slender means is telling on this mother of six children. The father is probably a skilled worker, possibly a clerk; the kitchen is the family living room. Note the bananas—a benefit of Empire—books and religious print and motto.

6.18 Child labour: a mother and daughters eke out a living from bristle-making in their kitchen. The wallpaper is peeling, and the table on the point of collapse, but the home is a good deal less poor than some, where the only furniture would have been orange boxes.

6.19 Independent old age: Granny Wilson, the oldest member of Sighthill United Free Church, Springburn, Glasgow, at home in 1901, with her kettle on the hob.

6.20 Grandmother, 1908: of those who lived to
seventy, the majority were widows living with their
own children or grandchildren.

6.21 Celebrating the first pension date at
Wickhambrook, Suffolk, 6 January 1908. Lloyd
George had introduced a pension of £13 a year,
means-tested and character-tested, and excluding
those on poor relief, for those who reached the age
of seventy. 'They were relieved of anxiety. They
were suddenly rich. Independent for life!', Flora
Thompson remembered of the cottagers. As they
went down to the Post Office to draw it, some were
at first in tears, others would mutter: ' "God bless
that Lord George!" (for they could not believe one
so powerful and munificent could be a plain "Mr")
and "God bless *you*, miss!".'

6.22 Old and bedridden in Crumpsall
Workhouse, Manchester. For the chronically rather
than acutely sick, the workhouses provided the
main hospital service, and especially for the old. By
the age of 75 almost one Edwardian in three was a
pauper, and the chances of dying in the workhouse
were still higher.

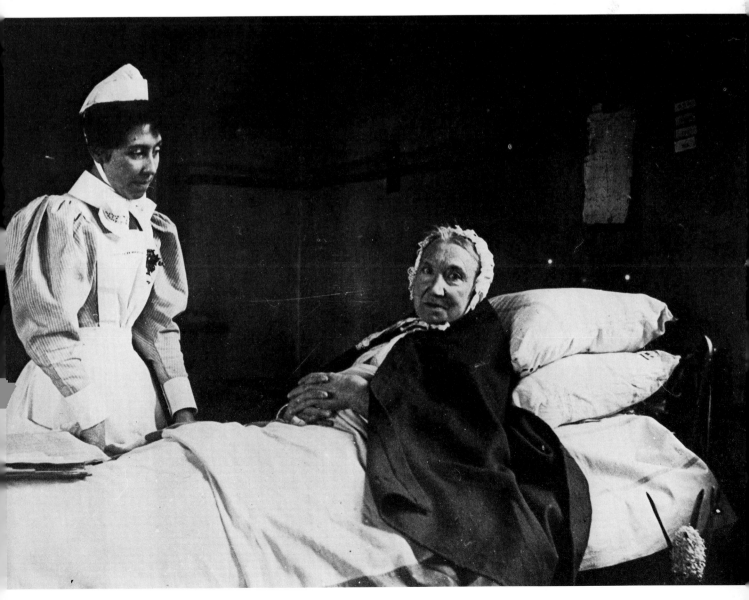

6.23 Working man's funeral: large crowds follow
the hearse of John Welsby, Yorkshire miner, to
Altofts Cemetery on 14 March 1908. He had died
as one of a special rescue team sent unsuccessfully
to try to save 26 miners trapped and killed
underground by a fire at Hamstead Colliery in the
Midlands, near Birmingham. Funeral insurance
was the most widespread saving in Edwardian
Britain; it allowed death in ordinary families to be
celebrated with much greater ceremony than any
passage in life itself.

LEISURE

The industrial revolution had made its own forms of leisure to match the discipline of the long factory working week. Pre-industrial leisure had been irregular, bucolic and often violent. By the late nineteenth century some of the most brutal sports, like bear-baiting and cock-fighting, had been almost stamped out. The pub licensing system was just beginning to control the outlets for drink. The weekend had become much more uniform: for most workers it began on Saturday afternoon, and few now kept the traditional custom of making a holiday of 'St Monday' too. In the industrial north, local factories had consolidated the old days off into a single 'wakes week', which allowed the families of better-paid workers a holiday by the seaside staying in a boarding house. This was the first heyday of Blackpool: the Victoria pier, the tower, the great wheel, the immense dance-rooms.

Dancing was one of the great crazes of the early twentieth century, a fervently seized chink in the armour of Edwardian repression. The poor danced 'The Lambeth Walk' to the tune of itinerant barrel organs in their own slum streets. The rich slid the new American foxtrot to black bands in the Ritz and the Savoy. Others just waltzed on the grass on a Bank Holiday outing, or when a travelling fair passed their way. There was no radio yet (although the gramophone had come) and Edwardians were used to making their own music. They whistled and sang in the streets and at work. It was the age of Elgar, of the Handel festival choirs and the colliery brass bands of Wales and the north, of family hymn-singing, of the mouth organ, the melodeon and the fiddle, of folk-song in the pubs.

Beer-drinking was the most widespread of all pleasures. Every Edwardian adult consumed on average six pints a week. Although starting to decline, drunkenness was still a serious problem, and the police brought over four thousand prosecutions weekly. But drinking was generally a more humdrum relaxation. Children fetched home beer in jugs. Women, especially in Wales and the north, were often unwelcome in pubs. For men, however, pubs everywhere offered comfort and warmth, and some useful work contacts too, as well as meeting places for savings clubs, union branches and sports clubs.

The most popular of all sports was already football, played in every street, and also the leading spectator sport. It had been systematised and made less dangerous with new national rules, through upper-class patronage. Cricket remained both a gentlemanly and popular sport; and a similar upper-class presence had regularised boxing, and prevented the extinction of blood sports like ratting and hunting. The maintenance of hunting, with stables and kennels, also demanded substantial wealth; and the same applied to other upper-class sports like racing, yachting—at that time with paid crews—and also sports like golf and motoring which were new fashions of the time. Among ordinary people an equally important change was the spread of quieter, more private interests. At home there was the Sunday paper, the allotment, the pigeon or the dog. In the towns the silent cinema had arrived to rival the beer-drinking music hall. And further afield, the countryside waited for the rambler and the bicyclist.

7.1 The congeniality of a drink and a game of cards in the back yard conveys something of the typical pub atmosphere too—of which, for both social and technical reasons, convincing photographs are rare. Despite powerful temperance campaigns, beer-drinking remained the commonest pleasure of the age, occupying the place today taken by cigarettes and television.

7.2 A country outing, c. 1906: no fear of the motorist yet. This Kodak photograph looks like a genuine snap by the third lady, who has left her bicycle against the bridge. The bicycle brought a tremendous new freedom for women—but each man holds on to his own map.

7.3 Home gardeners at Springburn, Glasgow: creative achievement, quiet, and contact with nature for the industrial worker.

7.4 Yorkshire picnic: the Leeds deputy town clerk and friends in Lindley Wood. With a menu of soup, meats, dessert, cheeses, accompanying wines and coffee, the simple outdoor life for the well-to-do was still quite complicated.

7.5 A Thames punting party near Boulter's Lock on Ascot Sunday, June 1912: this hamper must have taken some organising by the servants too. The men's hands are posed a little anxiously.

7.6 At the Bath Horse Show, September 1910. Horse racing was an aristocratic and also a popular sport, motoring a pleasure which only the wealthy could afford. Cars were craft-made masterpieces built to last—and to stand up to the hunting spirit of many of the first motorists.

7.7 London girls dancing to a street organ, 1902, a common sight in poor districts: 'heel and toe, double shuffle, glissade, battement, high kick. . . . They dance for sheer joy'.

7.8 Scottish couples dancing on the grass: one of the later photographs by George Washington Wilson of Aberdeen, who had built up one of Britain's leading picture postcard firms from the 1860s by developing the 'instantaneous' street view taken by a stereoscopic camera. He moved on to take industrial and rural work scenes too, and even made a special voyage in 1886 to make a unique record of the remote seabird-eating islanders of St Kilda.

7.9 Live music: on the beach at South Shields. Taken by the local commercial photographer, James Cleet.

7.10 Father and daughter at the sea, from a Kodak photograph, c. 1910. Day outings had become possible even for the town poor, much to the disapproval of a social commentator like Elizabeth Chesser who in 1913 noted that 'parents of neglected, half-starved children' often were among those who found 'money to spend in drink, music-halls and picture palaces, who cannot do without their trips and outings, their annual holidays to Blackpool . . .'.

7.11 Hastings in 1914: the wheels of the bathing machine indicate the modesty required for changing into swimming gear, but the relatively simple costumes and the mixed group suggest a more relaxed view of physical fun.

7.12 and 7.13   At the Nottingham Goose Fair, 1910: the helter-skelter and the joy wheel. Like other great fairs of the time, features included theatre and cinema shows, boxing booths and a menagerie as well as steam-powered novelties like the great wheel, the 'Brooklyn cake-walk' and the joy wheel.

7.14   First of the mass media: the Hackney Picture Palace, Mare Street, East London, showing the 'latest war news' soon after the outbreak of the First World War. Cinemas began to compete with music halls in most towns in the 1900s and over 4000 were to be open before the end of the war. Social reformers were made acutely anxious by the unsupervised audiences of young people in the dark. The 'amusing and instructive' programme also includes Miss Henny Porter as 'The Great Sinner' in *Chéri-Bibi*.

7.15 Golf had originated as a popular sport on common 'links' in Scotland, but it needed space, and by this date expensive equipment. Along with other British sports, it was exported to the corners of the Empire, but had less permanent impact than football or cricket.

7.16 Opening for Eton: the Hon. G. W. Lyttelton and Mr C. E. Lambert go in to bat at Lords, July 1900.

7.17 Nottinghamshire County Football Club players with their supporters, 1906. Already the prime spectator sport, football attracted weekly crowds of 20,000 in the big towns, and had become a cult with the young: 'Nothing is so hotly discussed or so accurately known'. Players were on the way to stardom: 'A most amazing knowledge is betrayed of the personal appearance, character, and moral weakness of each individual player'.

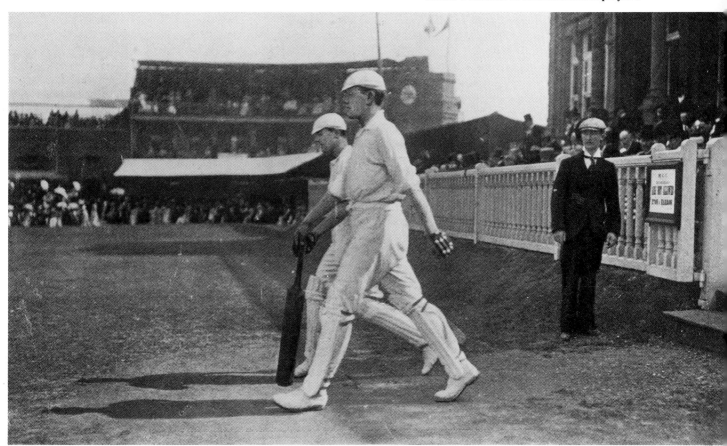

7.18 Cossetting the pet: another Kodak photograph of c. 1909. British sentimentality towards domestic animals went back at least a hundred years.

7.19 All the same, earlier tastes for brutal sports survived too: dogs await to dismember their prey before an assembly of 'ratting' enthusiasts in Old Oak Road, Hammersmith, on a Sunday morning, c. 1900.

THE MORAL ORDER

If most Edwardians were law-abiding, it was through consent rather than coercion. The Army could be brought in for emergencies, and was used to control a few major strikes, but most of it was stationed weeks away in India. The police were unarmed and localised, patrolling their beats on foot even after the advent of the motor criminal. Edwardians needed no personal documents—and even a national fingerprint system was not started until 1901. There was a smallish class of professional thieves and prostitutes; but those most often caught were drunks and tramps. Why then was a society whose inequalities were so evident accepted with such apparent ease?

Belief in the existing order was deep-seated. It was implanted in childhood. Education, despite the contrary example of a few 'progressive' pioneers, was less concerned with developing reason and creativity than with preparing children for their station in a hierarchical world. Corporal punishment was much harsher in schools than in most homes. Behind it loomed darker shadows: the fear of workhouse and prison for those who failed in this life, and of eternal punishment in the next.

Nearly all children went to Sunday School. Although in England, especially in towns, church attendance had fallen markedly, so that only a quarter of the adult population was in church or chapel on a typical Sunday, the majority of families still kept some church connection. Christian values were little challenged. A substantial proportion of schools were church-controlled. Locally, the clergy of the Church of England held their position as leaders of society. At the head of the Church stood the monarch. Piety and patriotism were intertwined. Both could draw immense popular enthusiasm on public occasions. Working-class Protestantism flourished especially in the Lancashire towns, stimulated by rivalry with the 'Popery' of Irish Catholic communities, whose backing for Home Rule threatened the very unity of the Empire.

Protestantism and the Empire were connected in another way too: in concern for individual moral and physical improvement. Religious campaigning for temperance, sexual purity and thrift also provided justification for political and social causes as diverse as self-help friendly societies, business enterprise, and even for the early socialism of the Independent Labour Party. In the Edwardian period it became linked with a new social anxiety: the needs of the Army and growing fears of German rivalry. If the Army's humiliation in the Boer War was not to be repeated, a fitter population was needed to provide recruits: and this revelation gave a new urgency to the health campaigning of socialists. Instruction in physical exercise, cleansing slum children of vermin, teaching girls housecraft and motherhood, were seen as contributions to a stronger nation. So was the new Boy Scouts movement, with its parallel Girl Guides founded to show 'How Girls Can Help Build the Empire'. As a youth movement the Scouts brought a fresh sense of outdoor adventure: to a generation already preparing to make—in the war to come—the supreme sacrifice for God and Empire.

8.1 The May Queen, rural idyll, celebrated in a London council school: learning to write in unison at Hugh Myddleton School, 1906. Nautical instruction also seems well drilled.

8.2 A housewifery class at Shoreditch Institute, east London, 1907. Some of these girls would be servants before marriage, so that the 'weekly routine' of cleaning, washing, starching and ironing for a 6-roomed household was a useful preparation for their station in life.

8.3 Entering assembly at Thomas Street council school, Limehouse, 1908.

8.4 Birmingham patriotism: proclamation of the new king in Victoria Square, 1910.

8.5 Established Church: the Bishop of Ely consecrates a churchyard extension at Chesterton, Cambridge, 1912. The Church of England baptised two thirds of all infants. Adult attendance had fallen most sharply in the industrial towns, least in the southern countryside.

8.6 'Watch and Pray': in Lancashire popular support for Protestantism was annually demonstrated by Whit Walks. The sexes quite commonly marched separately, as in this walk in Ashton Old Road, Openshaw, an industrial suburb of Manchester, c. 1910. In many families it was customary to buy their annual set of new clothes for the occasion. Besides church congregations, Mothers' Unions, Sunday Schools and men's classes, ambulance brigades, scouts and friendly societies also joined the Whit Walks in the cotton towns.

8.7 Thrift and self-improvement: a village friendly society day. At the edge of the green the brass band waits for the Foresters' procession to line up at Crookham, Hampshire, c. 1905.

8.8 Fitness in body and mind: Edwin Burden, Chipping Norton carpenter and chapel teacher, with his class at a Sunday School treat in 1912. Like many Nonconformists, he was an individualist who expressed a radical mission in his own special way: he was also composer of 'The March of the Witney Weightlifters'.

8.9 LEFT Boy scouts at camp with Baden-Powell at Humshaugh, August 1908. The scouting movement won over 200,000 members within its first dozen years. Its founder's aim was to teach its members to 'Be Prepared'—practically—in the event of war, invasion or other catastrophe, for strenuous outdoor manoeuvres. Its non-denominational moral education and outdoor entertainment provided the first serious rival to the churches' hold on the young through the Sunday School.

8.10 BELOW On the eve of war: officers' training camp for public school volunteers at Hagley Park, Birmingham, summer of 1913—from a postcard sent home to Cambridge by a Perse School boy.

8.11 ABOVE Reward for the deserving: a charity distribution of bread on the steps of St John's Church, Wolverhampton, c. 1900. Regular church attenders in the towns could hope for winter soup, coal and blankets, boots and clothes, and summer outings.

8.12 BELOW Penalty of crime: prisoners going to dinner at Wormwood Scrubs, 1903. Edwardian prisoners were kept in separate cells and forbidden to talk to each other, but prisons were less crowded, and cleaner than today. One reason was that the courts passed much shorter sentences than today: on average, under a fortnight.

8.13 Cleanliness: bathing verminous London schoolchildren at Sun Court Cleansing Station, 1912—part of the health movement to improve the nation's fitness.

8.14 Church visitor: a Methodist sister from Central Hall, Manchester, visiting a slum home in Ancoats.

8.15 OPPOSITE   Fool: nurse and patient in Crumpsall Workhouse, Manchester. Just a joke? What other role was open to a social discard?

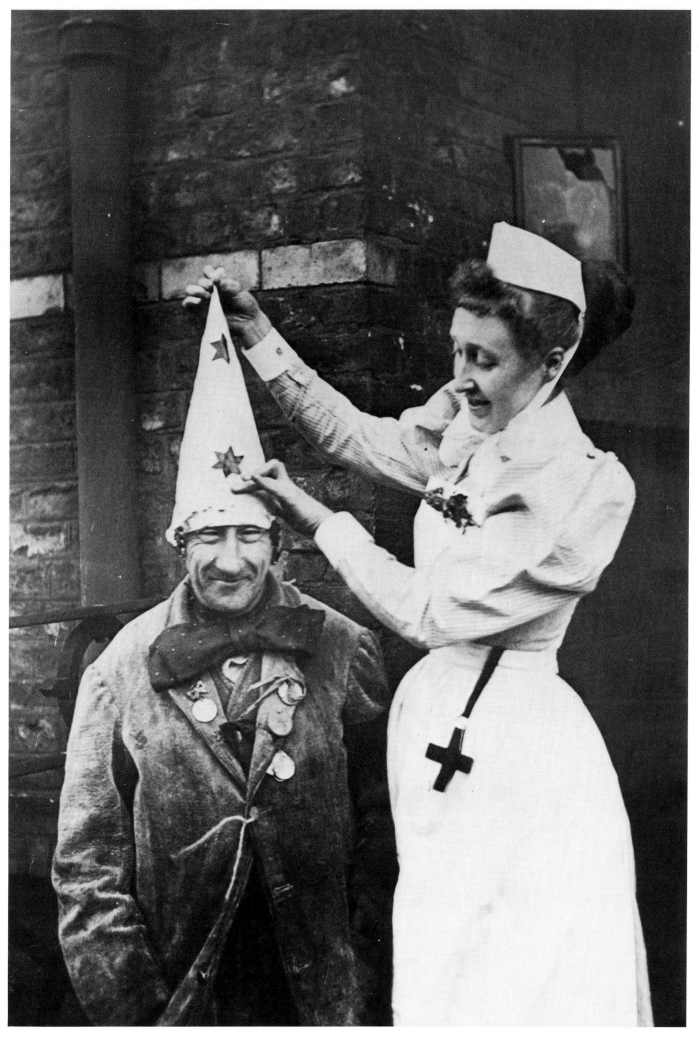

8.16   Children of the workhouse, Crumpsall:
frieze of deprivation.

THE EDWARDIAN CRISIS

British society seemed solid enough to most Edwardians. 'I firmly believed that kind of life was to continue for ever. Catastrophes might and did happen elsewhere . . .'. But even in Britain, especially in the last five years before the First World War, social conflict burst out into the open. The frustrated women's movement, repeatedly denied the vote, moved from dignified campaigning to the militancy of the suffragette movement. Respectable upper-class women were driven to window-breaking, picture-slashing, arson and self-mutilation. The politicians were trapped: the campaign forced them to confront the issue, and few of the arguments for denying women the right to vote now seemed sufficiently convincing. On the other hand, to concede to such forms of pressure was too much for male dignity.

At the same time, the old hunting and shooting aristocracy, rattled by the economic depression of agriculture and lured out by Lloyd George's threats of a new land tax, precipitated a parliamentary crisis by vetoing the budget for the first time in three hundred years. To bring down the Lords, a bargain had to be struck with the Nationalist MPs from Ireland, and Home Rule brought in. The Ulster Protestants answered by drilling an illegal volunteer army, under the slogan, 'Ulster Will Fight, and Ulster Will be Right'. The Conservatives, led by Bonar Law, backed them. When the government decided belatedly that it might need to disarm the volunteers, Bonar Law went on to incite the Army to the Curragh Mutiny. The First World War intervened before civil war broke out; but it was to follow.

Meanwhile the working classes had also broken into rebellion. From 1910 onwards a rash of strikes shook employers in town after town. Trade union membership leapt forward by a third in four years. Whole new groups of workers—the unskilled, clerks, women workers—for the first time formed permanent organisations. Troops were brought in to restore order in the South Wales mines strike of 1910, and for the first national railway strike in 1911, when more than once they opened fire and killed. The first national strike of 800,000 coal miners a year later was the biggest dispute yet seen, and forced Asquith as Prime Minister, reduced to tears, to rush a national minimum mine wage through Parliament within days. The exiled Lenin wrote in *Pravda*: 'Since the miners' strike the British proletariat *is no longer the same*. The workers have learned to fight. They have come to see the *path* that will lead them to victory.' He misjudged the situation: but so did Lloyd George, who told a City audience in 1914 that the coincidence of Irish civil conflict with labour unrest would create a crisis, 'the gravest with which any government has had to deal for centuries'. If he was wrong, not the least of reasons was his own achievement in pressing the negotiated settlement; and in laying the first steps of a welfare state which could blur the vividness of Edwardian inequality, harsh and splendid.

9.1 'Give Me Liberty or Give Me Death': the white column of suffragettes moves down Piccadilly behind the coffin of Emily Davison, killed by throwing herself under the king's horse at Tattenham Corner, Derby Day 1913.

9.2 Arrest outside Buckingham Palace as two hundred suffragettes attempted to induce the king to receive a deputation in support of votes for women, May 1914. Asquith, Prime Minister of the Liberal Government, had told the House of Commons: 'What seems to me to be the gist and core of the real question . . . is this—would our political fabric be strengthened; would our legislation be more respected; would our social and domestic life be enriched; would our standard of manners—and in manners I include the old-fashioned virtues of chivalry, courtesy and the reciprocal dependence and reliance of the two sexes—would that standard be raised and refined if women were politically enfranchised? . . . I answer it to the best of my knowledge in the negative. (Cheers.)'

9.3 Bonar Law, leader of the Conservative opposition, tells a rally at Blenheim Palace, seat of the Churchills outside Oxford, that if Home Rule was imposed on them Ulstermen 'would be justified in resisting by all means in their power, including force. . . . I can imagine no length of resistance to which Ulster will go in which I shall not be ready to support them.' By the end of 1912 the private army of Ulster Volunteers was 100,000 strong.

9.4 The independent Socialist candidate addressing a dinner hour meeting at the Reading by-election, 1913. The two main socialist parties had a membership together of around 70,000. Butler was a Marxist. Although not given official Labour backing, he polled a thousand votes out of 10,000.

9.5 The socialists led the campaigns for the unemployed, which proved particularly telling propaganda: a banner in Trafalgar Square, 1908. There was no dole until the end of the First World War.

EVICTED CHILDREN
AT DINNER
KINSLEY HOTEL
SEPT _____

9.6 and 9.7 Industrial confrontation: at Hemsworth Colliery, Yorkshire, 1600 miners came out on a wage dispute in the spring of 1905. In the late summer and early autumn the employers evicted 250 people from company-owned houses and they were forced to take refuge in tents. Relief funds were raised by appeals and travelling choirs of miners. The sympathetic landlord of the Kinsley Hotel gave some children sleeping room on his premises, where they are seen waiting to start a communal relief dinner. The miners held out for four years until they conceded defeat to the coalowners in June 1909.

9.8 and 9.9 The general transport strike, Liverpool, Red Sunday, 13 August 1911. Tom Mann, engineer, had been one of the socialist trio who led the London dockers to victory in the 1889 Dock Strike. Now, turned syndicalist, he addresses the vast crowd of strikers below St George's Hall. The two great banners symbolise the value of labour.

9.10 and 9.11   The meeting was followed by violence as police and troops dispersed the crowds with force. Later on, troops were stoned and a crowd attacked prison vans after arrests had been made. The troops opened fire and killed two people. Mann was imprisoned for issuing a 'Don't Shoot' appeal to soldiers. It was several days before police and troops had Liverpool again under control: seen here below, in a baton charge down Langsdale Street, and on the previous page, clearing the way down Scotland Road. Such displays could only buy time briefly. At one point there were eighteen separate strikes in Lancashire alone. During the railway strike troops were standing by to overawe disorder in more than thirty places. The labour unrest seemed unending. 'The public must be prepared for a conflict between Labour and Capital', declared *The Times*, 'upon a scale as has never occurred before.' Had not the First World War intervened, would that growing conflict have culminated in something like the General Strike of 1926, or in a different kind of confrontation? What would have been the outcome of the Edwardian crisis?